BEST
HOLIDAY
SWEETS &
TREATS

BEST HOLIDAY SWEETS & TREATS

GOOD AND SIMPLE FAMILY FAVORITES TO BAKE AND SHARE

DANIELLA MALFITANO

THE COUNTRYMAN PRESS

A DIVISION OF W. W. NORTON & COMPANY

INDEPENDENT PUBLISHERS SINCE 1923

For information about permission to reproduce selections from this book, write to
Permissions, The Countryman Press, 500 Fifth Avenue, New York, NY 10110

For information about special discounts for bulk purchases, please contact
W. W. Norton Special Sales at specialsales@wwnorton.com or 800-233-4830

Manufacturing by Versa Press

Library of Congress Cataloging-in-Publication Data

Names: Malfitano, Daniella, author.
Title: Best holiday sweets & treats : good and simple family favorites to
   bake and share / Daniella Malfitano.
Other titles: Best holiday sweets and treats
Description: New York, NY : The Countryman Press, a division of W. W. Norton &
   Company, [2016] | Series: Best ever | Includes index.
Identifiers: LCCN 2016031784 | ISBN 9781581574555 (pbk.)
Subjects: LCSH: Confectionery. | Cookies. | Holiday cooking. | LCGFT: Cookbooks.
Classification: LCC TX783 .M25 2016 | DDC 641.5/68—dc23 LC record available at
https://lccn.loc.gov/2016031784

The Countryman Press
www.countrymanpress.com

A division of W. W. Norton & Company, Inc.,
500 Fifth Avenue, New York, NY 10110
www.wwnorton.com

10 9 8 7 6 5 4 3 2 1

TO MY LOVING AND INCREDIBLE FAMILY.
YOU ARE EACH UNIQUELY AMAZING
AND I AM SO GRATEFUL
THAT I GET TO CALL YOU MINE.
THANK YOU FOR SUPPORTING ME
WITH EVERY ADVENTURE AND
FOR BELIEVING IN MY DREAMS.
HERE'S TO MORE CELEBRATING
AND EATING TOGETHER!
I LOVE YOU AND THIS ONE'S FOR YOU!

CONTENTS

Introduction

The recipes in this book are very special to me because these are the recipes I grew up enjoying every holiday season! Year after year and dessert after dessert, I came to appreciate the joys of holiday tradition and the food that comes along with it. Food is the center of most holidays, especially sweets! To me, these are the recipes that give every festive celebration its charm and are what makes the holidays such a special time of year. *Best Holiday Sweets & Treats* is a colorful and celebratory edition to the Best Ever Cookbook series. This cookbook has 50 scrumptious recipes in total, ranging from festive cookies to Santa's favorite squares and bars, to edible gifts and candies, to the sweet holiday classics! You might see goodies that you grew up with making or eating during the holidays, and others that might be new to you but are begging to be tried. The recipes in this book are simple to make and approachable for all types of cooks and all levels of baking skill, so fear not! Anyone and everyone can make them, and it is my hope that you will! Every sweet and treat in this book is fun to make, delicious to enjoy, and a perfect addition to your holidays. Now, go get your apron on and dive right in!

Enjoy!

With pleasure and an appetite,
Chef Daniella Malfitano

CHAPTER ONE
FESTIVE COOKIES

Gingersnap Cookies

Nothing says "Christmas" like the delicious scent of gingerbread. Spicy yet sweet, these cookies are a perfect balance of flavor. With dark molasses, cinnamon, and a pinch of salt, they'll keep you coming back for more. Their soft and chewy texture is just right for when you need a gingery burst of flavor and a little Yuletide spirit.

Makes 2 dozen cookies

1 cup granulated sugar

¾ cup unsalted butter, at room temperature

¼ cup dark molasses

1 large egg

1 teaspoon ground ginger

1 teaspoon ground cinnamon

2 teaspoons baking soda

½ teaspoon salt

2 cups all-purpose flour

¼ cup coarse raw cane sugar, for rolling cookies

Preheat the oven to 350°F. In a large bowl, cream the granulated sugar and butter together until light and fluffy. Add the molasses and egg and mix well. Add the ginger, cinnamon, baking soda, salt, and flour and mix until well combined.

Spoon out the dough into balls and form into 1½-inch balls. Roll the balls of dough in the raw cane sugar and then place on an ungreased baking sheet. Give them room; they will spread out while baking.

Bake for 8 to 10 minutes, or until they are slightly puffy.

> "Christmas is a season not only of rejoicing but of reflection."
> —Winston Churchill

Almond Fingers

With a perfect balance of powdered sugar and almond essence, these cookies are crumbly and nutty and give you just what you want when you need a sweet treat with an almond flair. They are easy to make and will become one of your favorite cookies this season. Just be warned, you may end up with powdered sugar on your lips and fingers!

Makes 2 to 3 dozen

1½ cups unsalted butter, at room temperature

¾ cup powdered sugar, plus more for rolling

¾ teaspoon salt

1½ cups finely ground almonds

1½ teaspoons almond extract

2 teaspoons pure vanilla extract

3 cups all-purpose flour, sifted

Preheat the oven to 325°F. In a large bowl, combine the butter, powdered sugar, and salt and mix until well combined. Add the ground almonds and the almond and vanilla extracts and mix. Add the flour gradually and continue to mix until a crumb mixture begins to form.

Shape balls of cookie dough into finger shapes. Place the dough 1 to 2 inches apart on an ungreased baking sheet. Bake for 10 to 15 minutes, or until light golden brown around the edges.

Gently transfer the cookies to a cooling rack and sprinkle with powdered sugar, then let cool completely. Once completely cool, gently roll each cookie in sifted powdered sugar before serving.

"Christmas is not a time nor a season, but a state of mind. To cherish peace and goodwill, to be plenteous in mercy, is to have the real spirit of Christmas."
—Calvin Coolidge

Nana's Butterhorns

You can thank Nana Rose for these! My nana would make these perfect butterhorns for all of the grandchildren at our annual Christmas Eve celebration, and I still have fond memories of watching her roll the dough and stuffing it with that sweet, walnutty filling. These buttery cookies are a perfect balance of spice and crunch, and can even be iced with a simple powdered sugar and buttermilk glaze for extra sweetness.

Makes 3 dozen cookies

4 cups unsalted butter, at room temperature, plus 3 tablespoons melted, for coating

2 cups all-purpose flour

1 large egg yolk

¾ cup buttermilk

½ cup chopped walnuts

½ cup granulated sugar, plus more for coating

1 teaspoon ground cinnamon

Line a baking sheet with parchment paper. In a large bowl, cut the butter into the flour. In a separate bowl, mix the egg yolk into the buttermilk and add to the flour mixture. If the dough seems too sticky, add more flour a little at a time. Form the dough into a big ball and wrap in plastic wrap. Refrigerate for at least 4 hours. When ready to bake, unwrap the dough and divide into three smaller balls.

In a small bowl, make the filling by mixing together the chopped walnuts, sugar, and cinnamon. Set aside.

Preheat the oven to 325°F. Scatter plenty of flour on a clean working surface. Using a rolling pin, roll out one ball of dough at a time. The dough should be fairly thin, about ⅛-inch thick, but not so thin that when you fill each cookie it would break open. Place a 6-inch round plate on the flattened dough and trace and cut out a circle. Push any dough that has been cut away in a pile to use later. Cut the circle into 4 to 6 pie-shaped wedges. Fill each wedge with 1 teaspoon of the walnut mixture starting at the large end, then roll into a small, crescent-shaped cookie.

Place the crescents on the baking sheet. Roll out and fill the remaining dough and place 1 inch apart on the baking sheet. Sprinkle with sugar before baking.

Bake for 20 minutes, or until light golden brown. Remove the cookies from the oven, brush with the melted butter, and dip into a bowl of sugar to coat.

Chocolate Walnut Balls

These can easily be a staple for your holiday baking lineup. They were one of the classic cookies that I enjoyed growing up as a kid and still enjoy today during Christmastime or for any family gathering of celebration. They have a soft texture and a full chocolaty flavor that is enhanced by cinnamon and walnuts. It's hard to have just one.

Makes 2 dozen cookies

1⅓ cups all-purpose flour

⅔ cup unsweetened cocoa powder

¾ teaspoon baking soda

⅛ teaspoon ground cinnamon

½ teaspoon salt

¾ cup unsalted butter, at room temperature

1¼ cups packed light brown sugar

1 teaspoon pure vanilla extract

2 large eggs

4 ounces semisweet chocolate chips

¾ cup walnuts, very finely chopped

Preheat the oven to 375°F and line a baking sheet with parchment paper. Sift the flour, cocoa powder, baking soda, cinnamon, and salt into a bowl.

In a separate bowl, beat together the butter, brown sugar, and vanilla until well combined. Add the eggs one at a time, beating until combined, then gradually add the dry mixture, mixing until everything is well incorporated. Add the chocolate chips and walnut pieces and stir to combine.

Scoop out heaping tablespoons of dough and roll between your hands to form uniform balls, then place on the prepared baking sheet, leaving at least 2 inches of space in between.

Bake for about 12 minutes, or until puffed. Remove from the oven and transfer the cookies to a cooling rack.

Crinkle Cookies

These cookies scream "Christmastime" with their chewy texture, chocolaty cocoa flavor, and beautiful powdered sugar–cracked texture. They really look beautiful on a platter. These were my sister Angelina's absolute favorite cookies, so I would trust her on this one!

Makes 3 dozen cookies

---

1 cup unsweetened cocoa powder

---

2 cups granulated sugar

½ cup vegetable oil

---

4 large eggs

⅛ teaspoon almond extract

---

3 teaspoons pure vanilla extract

---

2 cups all-purpose flour

---

2 teaspoons baking powder

---

1 teaspoon salt

½ cup powdered sugar, for dusting

In a large bowl, combine the cocoa powder, granulated sugar, and vegetable oil and mix well with a wooden spoon until smooth. Next, add the eggs and almond and vanilla extracts and mix again until everything is evenly combined.

In a small bowl, combine the flour, baking powder, and salt and mix well. Fold the dry ingredients into the wet ingredients and mix well to incorporate all the ingredients. Cover and refrigerate the dough for 2 hours.

Preheat the oven to 350°F. Line a baking sheet with parchment paper. Form heaping teaspoon-size balls of dough in your hands and then dip each dough ball into the powdered sugar. Place the sugar-coated dough balls 2 inches apart on the prepared baking sheet and bake for 10 minutes. Take out of the oven and before removing from the sheet, let the cookies cool slightly before transferring to a cooling rack to finish cooling.

Peanut Butter Kiss Cookies

If you want a perfect treat to please kids and "grown-up kids" at the same time, then look no further than these perfect Peanut Butter Kiss Cookies. These will bring you right back to your childhood. These sweet treats are a perfect flavor combination of peanut butter and milk chocolate.

Makes 4 dozen cookies

½ cup unsalted butter, at room temperature

¾ cup creamy peanut butter

⅓ cup granulated sugar, plus more for rolling

⅓ cup packed light brown sugar

1 large egg

2 tablespoons milk

1 teaspoon pure vanilla extract

1½ cups all-purpose flour

1 teaspoon baking soda

½ teaspoon salt

48 milk chocolate Hershey's Kisses, unwrapped

In a large bowl, cream together the butter, peanut butter, and sugars until well combined. Add the egg, milk, and vanilla and mix well.

In a separate bowl combine the flour, baking soda, and salt. Gradually beat the dry mixture into the peanut butter mixture. Refrigerate the dough for 30 minutes.

When ready to bake, preheat the oven to 375°F and shape the dough into 1-inch balls. Roll in additional granulated sugar, and arrange 2 inches apart on an ungreased baking sheet and flatten each ball slightly.

Bake for 8 to 10 minutes, or until lightly browned. Remove from the oven and immediately and gently press a chocolate kiss into the center of each cookie (the cookie will crack around the edges a little). Transfer the cookies to a cooling rack.

Snickerdoodles for Santa

Soft and chewy, these cookies are perfect in every way. Simple yet oh so delicious, the classic cinnamon and sugar flavor combination is a must during the holidays. And with ingredients that you may already have on hand, you can whip up a batch of these in no time. Feel free to make these larger than as formed in the recipe, for an even chewier cookie.

Makes 2 dozen cookies

1 cup unsalted butter, at room temperature

1½ cups plus 3 tablespoons granulated sugar, divided

2 large eggs

2¾ cups all-purpose flour

2 teaspoons cream of tartar

1 teaspoon baking soda

¼ teaspoon salt

1 tablespoon ground cinnamon

In a large bowl, mix the butter, 1½ cups of the granulated sugar and the eggs thoroughly. In a separate bowl, combine the flour, cream of tartar, baking soda, and salt. Blend the dry ingredients into the butter mixture. Chill the dough for 30 minutes.

Preheat the oven to 350°F. In a small bowl, mix together the remaining 3 tablespoons of sugar and the cinnamon. Scoop heaping tablespoon-size balls of dough into the cinnamon-sugar mixture. Gently roll each ball in the mixture.

Place the cookie balls 2 inches apart on an ungreased cookie sheet and flatten each ball slightly. Bake for 10 minutes. Remove from the oven and immediately transfer the cookies to a cooling rack.

Gingerbread Men

You can't get through the holiday season without making a batch of these. Perfect for baking and decorating with kids, these cookies will fill your home with the scent of ginger and will bring you right back to the good old days. Let your inner artist out and let your creative side loose when decorating your gingerbread men or women just the way you like.

Makes 3 dozen cookies

1 cup granulated sugar

½ cup molasses

½ cup water

1½ teaspoons ground ginger

2½ teaspoons ground cinnamon

1 teaspoon ground cloves

1 cup unsalted butter, at room temperature

4 cups all-purpose flour, plus more for dusting

1½ teaspoons baking soda

¼ teaspoon salt

ICING:

1½ cups powdered sugar

½ teaspoon pure vanilla extract

1 teaspoon light corn syrup

2 to 2½ tablespoons water

In a large saucepan over medium-high heat, stir together the granulated sugar, molasses, water, ginger, cinnamon, and cloves. Bring the mixture to a boil and stir until the sugar dissolves. Remove from the heat and add the butter. Stir occasionally until the butter is melted and incorporated, then let cool for 15 minutes.

In a medium-size bowl, sift together the flour, baking soda, and salt. Stir the flour mixture into the molasses mixture with a wooden spoon and mix well. Roll the dough into a ball and then flatten into a disk, wrap with plastic wrap, and refrigerate for 4 hours.

When ready to bake, preheat the oven to 375°F and line two baking sheets with parchment paper. Working with half of the dough at a time, roll out the dough to a ¼-inch thickness on a lightly floured work surface. Cut the dough into your desired gingerbread shapes. Transfer to the prepared baking sheet 2 inches apart. Bake for 8 to 10 minutes, until set and lightly browned. Remove from the oven and let the cookies cool on cooling racks before icing.

For the icing, in a medium-size bowl, whisk the powdered sugar, vanilla, corn syrup, and 2 tablespoons of water. It should have a thick consistency. Add more water if you want a thinner icing. Color portions of the icing as you'd like and decorate your cookies before serving.

Decorative Sugar Cookies

These adorable cookies not only will showcase your decorating skills, but will fulfill your cookie hunger for a delicious and classic sweet treat. When I was younger, I would beg my mother to get edible silver balls for decorations; now you can buy silver and gold flakes and sprinkles to make your cookies literally shine. Use store-bought frosting, or get fancy and make your own. Either way, gather the family around the table and have a decorating contest—whoever wins gets the last cookie!

Makes 2 to 3 dozen cookies

3 cups all-purpose flour, plus more for dusting

2 teaspoons baking powder

1 cup unsalted butter, at room temperature

1 cup granulated sugar

1 large egg

1 teaspoon pure vanilla extract

ICING:

1½ cups powdered sugar

½ teaspoon vanilla extract

1 teaspoon light corn syrup

2 to 2½ tablespoons water

In a large bowl, combine the flour and baking powder.

In a separate bowl, cream the butter and granulated sugar together, then add the egg and vanilla and mix well. Slowly incorporate the dry ingredients and mix just until well combined. Chill the dough for 1 hour.

Preheat the oven to 350°F. Line a baking sheet with parchment paper. Roll out dough onto a lightly floured work surface to your desired thickness. Cut out cookies using cookie cutters and place 1 inch apart on the prepared baking sheet. Bake for 10 to 12 minutes. Remove from the oven and transfer the cookies to cooling racks.

For the icing, whisk the powdered sugar, vanilla, corn syrup, and 2 tablespoons of water in a medium-size bowl. It should have a thick consistency. Add more water if you want a thinner icing. Color portions of the icing as you'd like and decorate your cookies before serving.

Chocolate-Dipped Coconut Macaroons

These cookies will come together quickly with only six ingredients. They are fun to decorate and will be ready in no time when you want something a little coconutty and chocolaty to enjoy and share with your loved ones. You can replace the dark chocolate with milk chocolate, or even white chocolate for an even sweeter treat.

Makes 2 dozen cookies

14 ounces sweetened shredded coconut

14 ounces sweetened condensed milk

1 teaspoon pure vanilla extract

2 extra-large egg whites, at room temperature

¼ teaspoon kosher salt

12 ounces dark or semisweet chocolate chips

Preheat the oven to 325°F. Line a baking sheet with parchment paper. In a large bowl, combine the coconut, sweetened condensed milk, and vanilla and mix well.

In the bowl of a stand mixer fitted with the whisk attachment, whip the egg whites and salt on high speed until they make medium-firm peaks. Carefully fold the whipped egg whites into the coconut mixture.

Drop heaping tablespoons of the cookie dough 1 inch apart onto the prepared baking sheet. Bake for 25 to 30 minutes, or until golden brown. Remove from the oven and let the cookies cool for 2 minutes, then transfer the cookies to a cooling rack.

Melt the chocolate in a microwave or in the top of a double boiler. Dip the bottom of each cookie into the melted chocolate and put back on the cooling rack. Drizzle the cookies with a few decorative stripes of chocolate on top, then let the chocolate dry and the cookies cool completely.

Jam Thumbprint Cookies

Who doesn't love jam thumbprint cookies? These are a perfect combination of buttery rich flavor with a sweet jam center. Enjoy them with any flavor jam you like, or make a batch with a combination of different jam centers for variation. I roll these cookies in walnuts before baking, but feel free to try them with finely chopped almonds or pecans, too, or leave the nuts off altogether for a simpler cookie with a more traditional soft and chewy butter cookie flavor.

Makes 2 dozen cookies

1½ cups all-purpose flour

1 teaspoon baking powder

½ teaspoon salt

1¼ cups unsalted butter, at room temperature

1 cup granulated sugar

1 large egg

1 teaspoon almond extract

½ cup walnuts, finely chopped

Raspberry jam

Preheat the oven to 350°F. In a medium-size bowl, whisk together the flour, baking powder, and salt. In a separate bowl, cream together the butter and sugar until well combined. Add the egg and almond extract and mix well. Gradually add the flour mixture and mix well.

Form heaping tablespoons of the dough and roll in the chopped walnuts. Place the dough balls 2 inches apart on an ungreased baking sheet and make an indentation using your thumb. Fill each indentation with ½ to 1 teaspoon of jam.

Bake for 15 minutes, rotating the baking sheet halfway through. Remove from the oven and allow the cookies to cool for 5 minutes on the baking sheet and then transfer them to a cooling rack.

Cocoa Peanut Butter Cookies

These cookies have a very mild flavor that is much less sweet than a traditional peanut butter or chocolate cookie. These have a subtle and sweet hint of cocoa and peanut butter mixed together in a perfect soft and chewy texture, perfect for when you want something simple and just enough to fulfill your cookie craving. These can be baked smaller than suggested for cookies that are a bit crispier.

Makes 2 to 3 dozen cookies

1 cup unsalted butter, at room temperature

¼ cup creamy peanut butter

1¼ cups granulated sugar

1 cup packed dark brown sugar

1 tablespoon pure vanilla extract

½ teaspoon salt

2 large eggs

2¼ cups all-purpose flour

¾ cup unsweetened cocoa powder

1½ teaspoons baking soda

Preheat the oven to 375°F. In a large bowl, cream together the butter, peanut butter, sugars, vanilla, and salt until well combined, then add the eggs and mix well.

In a separate medium-size bowl, combine the flour, cocoa powder, and baking soda. Gradually add the dry ingredients to the peanut butter mixture and mix well.

Scoop heaping tablespoons of cookie dough 2 inches apart onto an ungreased cookie sheet. Bake for 10 minutes, or until the cookies are slightly puffy. Remove from the oven and let cool slightly, then transfer the cookies to a cooling rack.

Soft Glazed Anise Cookies

I adore these soft little licorice-flavored cookies! These are an Italian American treat traditionally made for Christmas or other big celebrations. Perfect for any festive holiday celebration, these little gems are a delicate combination of sweet anise and soft butter cake. Decorate them as described or just simply glazed if you don't like sprinkles. If you've never had an anise-flavored cookie, you might be surprised by how delicious these are.

Makes 2 to 3 dozen cookies

3 large eggs

¾ cup granulated sugar

2 teaspoons anise extract

½ teaspoon pure vanilla extract

4 teaspoons baking powder

¾ cup vegetable oil

½ cup milk

4 cups all-purpose flour

Rainbow nonpareils (round sprinkles)

GLAZE:

2 cups powdered sugar

2 to 3 tablespoons milk

1 teaspoon pure vanilla extract

Preheat the oven to 350°F. Line a baking sheet with parchment paper. In a large bowl, beat together the eggs, granulated sugar, anise and vanilla extracts, and baking powder. In a separate bowl, combine the vegetable oil and milk and then add the flour and quickly mix well. Gradually add this mixture to the egg mixture and mix until well combined.

Scoop heaping tablespoons of dough into your hands and roll into smooth balls. Place about an inch apart on the prepared baking sheet. Bake for 10 to 12 minutes, or until the bottoms are slightly golden. Remove from the oven, then transfer the cookies to a cooling rack.

For the glaze, in a medium-size bowl, combine the powdered sugar, milk, and vanilla and mix well. Drop the cooled cookies into the glaze, then scoop out with a slotted spoon and return to the parchment-lined baking sheet. Top with nonpareils.

Butter Cookies

Oh, butter cookies! Butter cookies are everyone's favorite, especially during the holidays. This recipe is so simple yet so delicious, with a perfect combination of butter, sugar, and vanilla. Try shaping them with any shape from your cookie press, or make a combination of shapes in the same batch to make a homemade tin of these butter cookies.

Makes 3 to 4 dozen cookies

1 cup unsalted butter, at room temperature

⅔ cup granulated sugar

1 large egg

2 teaspoons pure vanilla extract

½ teaspoon salt

2¼ cups all-purpose flour

Preheat the oven to 375°F. In a bowl, combine the butter, sugar, egg, vanilla, and salt and mix well until creamy. Gradually add the flour and mix well.

Place the dough into a cookie press fitted with a star template or any other shape that you desire. Press the cookies 2 inches apart onto an ungreased baking sheet and bake for 10 to 12 minutes, or until cookies are light golden brown. Let the cookies sit for 5 minutes on the baking sheet before transferring to a cooling rack.

"'Tis merry 'neath the mistletoe,
When holly-berries glisten bright;
When Christmas fires gleam and glow,
When wintry winds so wildly blow,
And all the meadows round are white—
'Tis merry 'neath the mistletoe!"

—"A Christmas Carol" by J. Ashby-Sterry

Iced Pumpkin Cookies

Pumpkin spice is a fan favorite for a reason, and the love doesn't disappear with the fall leaves. These warm and spicy holiday treats are a must-have for any holiday gathering. They have a cake-like consistency and a full flavor that works perfectly with the thick icing. Serve these to a crowd and watch the cookies disappear quickly.

Makes 3 dozen cookies

2½ cups all-purpose flour

1 teaspoon baking powder

1 teaspoon baking soda

1 tablespoon pumpkin pie spice

½ teaspoon salt

½ cup unsalted butter, at room temperature

1½ cups granulated sugar

1 cup pure pumpkin puree

1 large egg

1 teaspoon pure vanilla extract

ICING:

2 cups powdered sugar

1 tablespoon unsalted butter, melted

2 to 3 tablespoons milk

1 tablespoon pure vanilla extract

Line a baking sheet with parchment paper. In a medium-size bowl, combine the flour, baking powder, baking soda, pumpkin pie spice, and salt and mix well. In a separate large bowl, combine the butter and granulated sugar and mix well. Add the pumpkin, egg, and vanilla and mix until smooth and uniform, then gradually mix in the dry ingredients until combined.

Refrigerate the dough for 30 minutes. When ready to bake, preheat the oven to 350°F and scoop heaping tablespoons of dough 1 inch apart onto the prepared baking sheet and bake for 15 to 18 minutes, or until slightly golden brown. Remove from the oven and transfer the cookies to cooling racks to cool completely before frosting.

For the icing, in a bowl, combine the powdered sugar, melted butter, milk, and vanilla and mix well until a smooth icing forms. Ice the cooled cookies before serving.

Tip: Pumpkin pie spice is a combination of classic baking spices and can be found in the spice section of most supermarkets and specialty markets.

Vanilla Crescents

These festive cookies are a perfect elegant addition during the holidays or really anytime of the year for a celebratory occasion. They go perfectly with a cup of coffee or tea. The almond meal in this recipe gives these cookies a particular coarse and crisp consistency that I really love.

Makes 2 dozen cookies

½ cup unsalted butter, room temperature

¼ cup granulated sugar

½ teaspoon pure vanilla extract

1 cup all-purpose flour

½ cup almond meal

¼ teaspoon salt

Powdered sugar, for dusting

Preheat the oven to 350°F. In a large bowl, combine the butter and granulated sugar and mix with a wooden spoon until light and fluffy, then mix in the vanilla. In a separate medium-size bowl, combine the flour, almond meal, and salt. Pour the dry ingredients into the butter mixture and mix well.

Divide the dough into two pieces and, on a floured cutting board, roll each portion into a 24-inch rope. Cut each rope crosswise into twelve 2-inch pieces and simply shape each piece into a crescent.

Place the cresents 1 inch apart on an ungreased cookie sheet and bake for 10 to 12 minutes, or until a bit golden. Let the cookies sit for 5 minutes on a baking sheet before transferring to a cooling rack. Once the cookies are cool, dust them with a generous coating of powdered sugar.

> "Then the Grinch thought of something he hadn't before! What if Christmas, he thought, doesn't come from a store. What if Christmas . . . perhaps . . . means a little bit more!"
>
> —Dr. Seuss, *How the Grinch Stole Christmas!*

Black & White Cookies

These old-school black-and-white cookies are a perfect combination of a soft and tender cookie-shaped cake frosted with delicious, thick chocolate and vanilla icing. This sweet treat is perfect for sharing with family and friends during the holidays, and is a festive addition to your regular holiday baking offerings.

Makes 2 dozen cookies

4 cups cake flour

½ teaspoon baking powder

½ teaspoon salt

1 cup unsalted butter, at room temperature

1¾ cups granulated sugar

2 large eggs, at room temperature

2 teaspoons pure vanilla extract

1 cup milk

ICING:

2 ounces unsweetened dark chocolate, finely chopped

⅓ cup water

¼ cup light corn syrup

5 cups powdered sugar

½ teaspoon pure vanilla extract

Preheat the oven to 375°F. Line a baking sheet with parchment paper. In a large bowl, whisk together the flour, baking powder, and salt. In a separate large bowl, combine the butter and granulated sugar and mix well for several minutes, until the mixture is light in color, creamy, and airy. Add the eggs and vanilla and mix to combine. Gradually add the flour mixture and the milk a little bit at a time and mix until just combined.

Scoop ¼ cup of dough 2 inches apart onto the prepared baking sheet and use wet fingers to gently press each mound of dough into a 2-inch circle. Bake for 18 to 20 minutes, or until the cookies are light golden brown. Remove from the oven and let cool slightly, then transfer the cookies to a cooling rack.

While the cookies cool, make the icing: Melt the chocolate in a microwave-safe bowl in the microwave or in the top of a double boiler. In a medium-size saucepan over medium heat, bring the water and corn syrup to a boil. Remove from the heat and whisk in the powdered sugar and vanilla. Transfer ¾ cup of the icing to the bowl of melted chocolate and whisk to combine. Transfer the remaining vanilla icing to a small bowl.

Place a cooling rack over a baking sheet to catch any excess icing. Use a small offset spatula to spread about 2 tablespoons of the vanilla icing onto half of each cookie. Place the cookies on the cooling rack for 10 minutes to set. Then, again using a small offset spatula, spread the chocolate icing on the remaining half of each cookie. Let the cookies set for 30 minutes before serving or storing.

Cinnamon Stars

Aren't these adorable? I think so, too. These delicious little cookies have a nutty flavor that pairs well with their white citrusy icing. The stars are perfect for the holidays and can be made into any shape that you like, so try them with any cookie cutters that you have on hand.

Makes 3 dozen cookies

3 large egg whites

Pinch of salt

2 cups powdered sugar, plus more for rolling

1½ tablespoons ground cinnamon

½ tablespoon freshly squeezed lemon juice

3 cups almonds

In a large bowl, whisk the egg whites and salt until they are thick and frothy. Gradually add the powdered sugar and mix well. Set aside ⅓ cup of the mixture to use as frosting.

Gently stir the cinnamon and lemon juice into the egg white mixture. Grind the almonds in a food processor to a fine chop and add to the rest of the mixture, mixing with a spatula just until well combined. Chill the dough for 1 hour before rolling and shaping.

Preheat the oven to 475°F. Line a baking sheet with parchment paper. Dust a work surface with powdered sugar and roll out the dough to about ½-inch thick. Use a star cookie cutter to shape stars, then arrange 1 inch apart on the prepared baking sheet.

Stir the frosting and then gently coat each star. Bake the cookies for 5 minutes. Remove from the oven and transfer the cookies to a cooling rack. Allow to cool before serving.

"One of the most glorious messes in the world is the mess created in the living room on Christmas day. Don't clean it up too quickly."

—Andy Rooney

Holiday Madeleines

These soft cookies are considered little cakes and are simply perfect for your dessert craving. They look tricky, but come together in a flash (no one has to know just how easy it was). They have a mild vanilla flavor and are not overly sweet, making them great with tea or your creamiest hot cocoa.

Makes 2 dozen cookies

1 cup all-purpose flour, plus more for dusting

½ teaspoon baking powder

¼ teaspoon salt

3 large eggs, at room temperature

½ cup granulated sugar

1 tablespoon honey

2 teaspoons pure vanilla extract

½ cup unsalted butter, melted, plus more for pan

Powdered sugar, for dusting

In a small bowl, sift together the flour, baking powder, and salt. In a separate bowl, combine the eggs, granulated sugar, honey, and vanilla and beat until the mixture is light and fluffy. Gradually add the flour mixture to the egg mixture and fold in the melted butter.

Cover the bowl of dough with plastic and chill for 1 hour.

Preheat the oven to 375°F. Prepare a Madeleine pan or pans by generously buttering and then flouring the molds, tapping out any excess flour. Fill the molds about three-quarters full and bake for 8 to 10 minutes. The edges will be golden brown and the centers will be spongy. Remove from the oven and invert the pan over a cooling rack and tap to release the Madeleines. Once the cookies are cool, dust with powdered sugar before serving.

Auntie Cici's Biscotti

These cookies have the traditional flavor of classic Italian biscotti, with the addition of a subtle lemon essence. These can be made with any combination of nuts and dried fruit, such as walnut and dates, pistachios and dried cherries, or pine nuts and currants. You can also replace the lemon extract with almond or vanilla, for a different flavor.

Makes 4 dozen medium-size biscotti

½ cup unsalted butter, at room temperature

1 cup granulated sugar

2 large eggs

1 tablespoon pure vanilla extract

2 teaspoons lemon extract

2½ cups all-purpose flour

2½ teaspoons baking powder

½ teaspoon salt

1 cup sliced almonds

1 (6-ounce) package dried cranberries

Preheat the oven to 350°F. In a large bowl, cream the butter and sugar together. Add the eggs and mix until creamy, then add the vanilla and lemon extracts and mix thoroughly. In a separate medium-size bowl, mix the flour, baking powder, and salt. Gradually add the flour mixture to the butter mixture a little at a time and mix just to combine. Fold in the sliced almonds and cranberries and mix well.

Separate the dough into three equal portions. Form each portion into a long loaf. Line two baking sheets with parchment paper. Place two of the loaves on one prepared pan and the third loaf on the other. Bake for about 20 minutes.

Remove from the oven and, using two spatulas, lift each loaf onto a cutting board. Lower the oven temperature to 300°F. While the loaves are still warm, using a serrated knife, carefully slice each loaf diagonally to cut cookies about

¾-inch thick. Lay the cut cookies on their side on the lined baking sheets and toast in the oven for 10 to 15 minutes, turning halfway through to evenly toast both cut sides of the biscotti. Remove from the oven and transfer the biscotti to cooling racks and let cool completely.

Caramel Sandwich Cookies

A perfect combination of buttery wafers and a caramel center, these sandwich cookies are nice to have around for the holidays. These are a staple in South America during the holidays and in some areas all year-round. I know because I couldn't get enough of them when I lived in Argentina! If you don't have time to make the caramel sauce, then save time with a bottle of store-bought caramel or dulce de leche.

Makes 1 dozen sandwich cookies

¾ cup all-purpose flour

⅓ cup cornstarch

¼ teaspoon baking powder

⅛ teaspoon salt

6 tablespoons unsalted butter, at room temperature

¼ cup granulated sugar

2 large egg yolks

¼ teaspoon pure vanilla extract

CARAMEL:

4 tablespoons unsalted butter, at room temperature

⅓ cup firmly packed light brown sugar

Pinch of kosher salt

2 tablespoons heavy whipping cream

Preheat the oven to 350°F. Line a baking sheet with parchment paper. In a medium-size bowl, combine the flour, cornstarch, baking powder, and salt and mix well. In a separate large bowl, cream together the butter and the granulated sugar until fluffy, then add the egg yolks and vanilla and mix well. Gradually add the dry ingredients to the butter mixture and fold just to combine.

On a lightly floured work surface, roll out the dough into a large circle. Using a small, round cookie cutter, cut 24 rounds, rerolling the scraps if necessary. Arrange the circles ½ inch apart on the prepared baking sheet. Bake the cookies for 10 to 12 minutes, or until a very pale brown. Remove from the oven and transfer the cookies to a cooling rack.

While the cookies cool, make the caramel. In a small saucepan, combine the butter, the brown sugar, and the pinch of salt over medium heat. Cook this mixture for 2 to 3 minutes, or until it begins to bubble and thicken, then remove it from the heat. Gradually whisk the cream into the caramel mixture and stir until well combined and uniform in color. Chill the caramel for 15 minutes. Sandwich the cookies with about 1 teaspoon of caramel sauce per sandwich before serving.

Cranberry Macadamia Nut Cookies

These soft, festive, and delicious cookies are perfect for macadamia nut lovers! They have a great tart and nutty balance. This sweet treat is just perfect for Santa, so be sure to leave a few out for him the night he stops by.

Makes 2 dozen cookies

2¼ cups all-purpose flour

1 teaspoon baking soda

1 teaspoon baking powder

1 teaspoon salt

1 cup unsalted butter, at room temperature

1 cup light brown sugar

1 cup granulated sugar

2 teaspoons pure vanilla extract

2 large eggs

1½ cups cranberries

2 cups macadamia nuts, coarsely chopped

Preheat the oven to 375°F. Line a baking sheet with parchment paper. In a medium-size bowl, combine the flour, baking soda, baking powder, and salt and mix well. In a separate large bowl, cream together the butter and sugars until fluffy. Next, add the vanilla and eggs and mix well. Gradually add the dry ingredients to the butter mixture and mix just until well combined, then gently fold in the cranberries and macadamia nuts.

Using a big spoon, arrange heaping scoopfuls of dough 2 inches on the prepared baking sheet. Bake for 10 to 12 minutes, or until the bottoms of the cookies are lightly browned. Remove from the oven and gently transfer the cookies to a cooling rack or serve warm right out of the oven for Santa.

Chocolate Christmas Crackles

These crackles are a more sophisticated version of classic crisp rice cereal treats. With the addition of chocolate, they are great for any occasion, casual, formal, and anything in between. Presented on a platter, these treats can be passed around the room to your guests, or arranged with other dessert offerings to mix up your usual dessert spread.

Makes 2 dozen cookies

6 tablespoons unsalted butter

1 (10½-ounce) bag mini marshmallows

¼ cup unsweetened cocoa powder

4 ounces semisweet chocolate chips

8 cups crisp rice cereal

Lightly grease foil cupcake wrappers. In a stockpot, combine the butter and marshmallows over medium heat. Once the butter and marshmallows begin to melt, add the cocoa powder and chocolate chips and stir until everything is well combined and melted together. Remove the pot from the heat and mix in the crisp rice cereal. Gently fold this mixture just until everything is well combined.

Drop 3- to 4-tablespoon mounds of the mixture into the prepared cupcake wrappers. Let sit for at least 1 hour to set before serving.

"My idea of Christmas, whether old-fashioned or modern, is very simple: loving others. Come to think of it, why do we have to wait for Christmas to do that?"
—Bob Hope

Eggnog Cookies

These buttery cookies define the flavors of the holidays. The eggnog and macadamia nuts are a wonderful combination, giving richness and crunch. Cut them into any shapes that you like, although the stars are perfect for Christmastime. These cookies are a fun project to make with kids, especially since you can have them make and decorate with the frosting and sprinkle with chopped nuts.

Makes 3 dozen cookies

1 cup unsalted butter, at room temperature

½ cup granulated sugar

½ teaspoon kosher salt

½ teaspoon pure vanilla extract

2 large egg yolks

2¼ cups all-purpose flour, plus more for dusting

ICING:

2 ounces cream cheese, softened

4 tablespoons unsalted butter, at room temperature

2 tablespoons eggnog

1 cup powdered sugar

¼ cup macadamia nuts, chopped, for sprinkling

In a large bowl, cream together the butter, granulated sugar, salt, and vanilla until fluffy. Beat in the egg yolks and mix until well combined. Gradually add the flour and mix until everything comes together in a sticky ball. Wrap the dough in plastic wrap and chill for at least 1 hour.

Preheat the oven to 375°F. Line 2 baking sheets with parchment paper. Roll out the dough on a lightly floured work surface. Using any shaped cookie cutter that you like, cut shapes from the dough, rerolling the scraps as needed. Arrange the cookies 1 inch apart on the prepared cookie sheets and bake for

11 to 13 minutes, or until they are slightly puffed. Remove from the oven and transfer the cookies to a cooling rack.

For the icing, in a large bowl, cream together the cream cheese and butter until completely smooth. Next, add the eggnog and mix again. Gradually add the powdered sugar and mix well until the icing is smooth. Frost each cookie, then sprinkle a bit of nuts onto the center of each to decorate.

Christmas Shortbread

This classic shortbread requires only three ingredients and is simple to put together. The cookies have a festive, traditional look to them that will add elegance to your holiday dessert table. I love shortbread cookies because they have a plain and buttery flavor that is not too sweet but is very rich and fulfilling. I especially love to enjoy these cookies with a tall glass of cold milk. It's heaven!

Makes 2 dozen cookies

2 cups unsalted butter, at room temperature

1 cup packed light brown sugar

3¾ cups all-purpose flour

Preheat the oven to 325°F. In a large bowl, cream together the butter and brown sugar until fluffy. Add the flour to the butter mixture and mix just until well combined.

Drop the entire bowlful of dough on a lightly floured work surface and knead for 3 to 4 minutes until the dough becomes soft and supple.

Roll out the dough to a ½-inch thickness. Cut into two dozen rectangular strips. Using a toothpick, prick each shortbread dough rectangle with several decorative holes, then arrange 1 inch apart on an ungreased baking sheet. Bake for 20 to 25 minutes. Remove from the oven and gently transfer the cookies to a cooling rack.

"I heard the bells on Christmas Day
Their old, familiar carols play,
And wild and sweet
The words repeat
Of peace on earth, good-will to men!"

—Henry Wadsworth Longfellow

Mrs. Claus's Double Chocolate Cookies

Perfect for chocolate lovers, these cookies are hard not to love. They have a very rich and delicious chocolate flavor from the cocoa powder and chocolate chips and will be sure to feed your chocolate craving. Try making these cookies with peanut butter, butterscotch, or mint chocolate chips for a different flavor variation that is just as delicious. Mrs. Claus likes them all!

Makes 1½ dozen cookies

- 1 cup unsalted butter, at room temperature
- 1½ cups granulated sugar
- 2 teaspoons pure vanilla extract
- 2 large eggs
- 2⅔ cups all-purpose flour
- ½ cup unsweetened cocoa powder
- 1 teaspoon baking soda
- ½ teaspoon salt
- 12 ounces milk chocolate chips

Preheat the oven to 350°F. Line a baking sheet with parchment paper. In a large bowl, cream together the butter, sugar, and vanilla until fluffy. Add the eggs and mix well. In a separate medium-size bowl, combine the flour, cocoa powder, baking soda, salt, and chocolate chips. Add the dry ingredients to the butter mixture and mix just until everything is combined.

Scoop large heaping tablespoons of the dough onto the prepared cookie sheet. Bake for 12 to 14 minutes or until just slightly puffed. Remove from the oven and let cool for 5 minutes before gently transferring the cookies to a cooling rack.

Soft Peppermint Meltaway Cookies

Peppermint meets a soft cookie and together they make perfection. These soft cookies are the essence of Christmastime with their crushed candy cane coating. They have a very soft and delicate consistency, with a bright peppermint flavor that will literally melt in your mouth. After you coat them with icing, add as much or as little crushed candy cane bits as you'd like, depending on your crowd.

Makes 4 dozen cookies

2 cups unsalted butter, at room temperature

1 cup powdered sugar

1 teaspoon peppermint extract

2½ cups all-purpose flour

1 cup cornstarch

¾ cup crushed peppermint candy canes

ICING:

4 tablespoons unsalted butter, at room temperature

¼ cup milk, plus more if needed

¼ teaspoon peppermint extract

3 cups powdered sugar

In a large bowl, cream together the butter, powdered sugar, and peppermint extract until fluffy. In a separate medium-size bowl, combine the flour and cornstarch. Gradually add the dry ingredients to the butter mixture and mix well just until everything is combined. Chill the dough in the bowl for 30 minutes.

Preheat the oven to 350°F. Scoop heaping tablespoons of the dough 2 inches apart onto an ungreased cookie sheet and bake for 8 to 10 minutes. Remove from the oven and let sit for 5 minutes before gently transferring the cookies to a cooling rack.

For the icing, in a medium-size bowl, combine the butter, milk, peppermint extract, and powdered sugar in a medium bowl. Mix well until the icing is soft enough to be spreadable. If the icing is too thick, then add more milk. Spread over the tops of the cookies and immediately sprinkle with candy cane bits.

CHAPTER TWO

SANTA'S FAVORITE SQUARES & BARS

Holiday Pecan Brownie Squares

You've got to try these enhanced pecan brownies for the holidays. They are a perfect combination of rich chocolaty flavor and nutty pecans that will be a simple yet delicious ending to any rustic holiday meal. And while you're at it, wash them down with a cup of hot cocoa or warm eggnog, to put yourself in the holiday spirit.

Makes 1 dozen squares

⅔ cup all-purpose flour

1½ teaspoons baking powder

½ teaspoon salt

3 cups chopped dark chocolate

1½ cups roughly chopped milk chocolate

1 cup unsalted butter

3 large eggs

1½ cups granulated sugar

1 tablespoon instant espresso powder

1 tablespoon pure vanilla extract

2 cups pecans, half chopped and half whole

Preheat the oven to 350°F. Line a 9 x 13-inch baking pan with foil extending over the sides and spray the foil with cooking spray. In a medium-size bowl, sift together the flour, baking powder, and salt and set aside. In a heatproof bowl or top of a double boiler, combine the two chocolates and butter, and place over a pot of simmering water. Stir constantly until the mixture is completely melted, then remove from the heat and let cool.

In a separate large bowl, combine the eggs, sugar, espresso powder, and vanilla. Gradually add the chocolate mixture to the egg mixture and mix well to combine. Fold the flour mixture into the egg mixture. Add the cup of chopped pecans and fold into the batter. Pour the mixture into the prepared baking pan and sprinkle the cup of whole pecans evenly on top of the mixture.

Bake for 18 to 20 minutes, or until a toothpick inserted into the center of the brownies comes out clean. Remove from the oven. Allow to cool before using the edges of the foil to lift from the baking pan and slicing into squares for serving.

Cranberry Bliss Bars

These delicious bars have layers of flavor, from the rich buttery base to the tart cranberries and the white chocolate sweetness. These look great served on platters and will be a showstopper as the end to any holiday meal. Cut them into smaller square pieces for bite-size portions, or enjoy them sliced on the bias for an elegant presentation.

Makes 18 bars

1¼ cups packed brown sugar

½ teaspoon salt

¾ cup unsalted butter, at room temperature

3 large eggs

1½ teaspoons pure vanilla extract

1½ cups all-purpose flour

½ teaspoon baking powder

½ teaspoon ground ginger

1½ cups dried cranberries, divided

4 ounces white chocolate chips

FROSTING:

4 ounces cream cheese, softened

2 cups powdered sugar

4 teaspoons freshly squeezed lemon juice

1 teaspoon pure vanilla extract

WHITE CHOCOLATE DRIZZLE:

2 ounces white chocolate chips

Preheat the oven to 350°F. Line a 12 x 16-inch baking sheet with parchment paper. In a large bowl, cream together the brown sugar, salt, and butter and mix until fluffy. Add the eggs and vanilla and mix well. In a separate medium-size bowl, combine the flour, baking powder, and ginger and mix well. Gradually add the dry mixture to the butter mixture and mix well, then fold in 1 cup of the dried cranberries and the white chocolate chips. Pour the batter onto the prepared baking sheet and spread evenly with a spatula, or gently tap the cookie sheet on a flat surface to spread the mixture out. Bake for 18 to 20 minutes, or until the middle is baked through and springs back when you touch it. Remove from the oven.

For the frosting, in a medium-size bowl, combine the cream cheese, powdered sugar, lemon juice, and vanilla and mix well until smooth and creamy.

For the white chocolate drizzle, place the white chocolate chips in a microwave-safe bowl in the microwave for about 30 seconds to melt, or melt in the top of a double boiler. Transfer the melted chocolate to a resealable plastic bag. Squeeze all the chocolate to one lower corner of the bag and snip a tiny bit off the corner, to create a piping bag.

Spread the frosting over the cooled crust, then sprinkle with the remaining ½ cup dried cranberries. Drizzle the melted white chocolate over the top in a decorative fashion, then let the bars set for 1 hour in the refrigerator before slicing diagonally into triangles.

Pear Raisin Strudel Squares

This is a delicious dessert that looks a lot more difficult to prepare than it really is. Your guests will appreciate this sweet and elegant ending to their meal. Or perhaps serve this as part of the meal for any festive holiday breakfast or brunch. The strudel is very easy to prepare and can be made in advance and reheated before serving, but you probably won't be able to wait to eat it if you try!

Makes 1 dozen squares

¼ cup granulated sugar

2 tablespoons all-purpose flour

½ teaspoon ground cinnamon

⅛ teaspoon freshly grated nutmeg

4 pears, peeled, cored, and thinly sliced

¼ cup raisins

1 (17.3-ounce) package puff pastry (2 sheets), thawed

2 large eggs, beaten

2 tablespoons water

2 tablespoons powdered sugar, for dusting

Preheat the oven to 375°F. Line a baking sheet with parchment paper. In a large bowl, combine the granulated sugar, flour, cinnamon, and nutmeg and mix well. Add the pears and raisins and toss to coat.

Working on a flat surface or cutting board, unfold the pastry sheets and roll out with a rolling pin to flatten each out just a bit, making sure to keep them the same size and dimensions. Place one of the flattened pastry sheets on the prepared baking sheet and spoon the pear mixture onto the pastry, spreading the filling all the way to the edge. Place the other flattened sheet of pastry over the filling.

In a small bowl, make an egg wash by beating together the eggs and water. Brush the top pastry with the egg wash. Cut several slits in the top of the

pastry to let air escape while baking. Bake for 25 to 30 minutes, or until the pastry is light golden brown. Remove from the oven. Let the pastry cool a bit before sifting with powdered sugar. Once the pastry has cooled for 15 minutes, slide onto a cutting board and cut into squares for serving. Dust with more powdered sugar before serving, if you'd like.

Rocky Road Christmas Crunch Bars

These bars have a great combination of flavors that sing together like the carolers at your front door. The graham crackers add a honey-flavored crunch, while the mini marshmallows give a gooey sweetness and the fudge hosts a smooth base and texture, all in one bite. These bars are crowd-pleasers all around. Make a batch for your family to try and you'll be baking these all season long.

Makes 14 to 18 bars

¼ cup whole walnuts

1½ cups broken-up graham crackers

1½ cups mini marshmallows

⅔ cup powdered sugar, divided

½ cup plus 2 tablespoons milk, at room temperature, divided

12 ounces semisweet chocolate chips

3 tablespoons unsalted butter, at room temperature

Line an 8-inch square baking pan with foil, then grease the foil. In a large bowl, combine the walnuts, graham cracker pieces, marshmallows, ½ cup of the powdered sugar, and 2 tablespoons of the milk and stir to mix.

In a small saucepan, combine the remaining ½ cup milk and remaining powdered sugar, and the chocolate chips and butter and place over low heat. Stirring constantly, heat until the chocolate and butter are melted. Pour only half of this mixture over the graham cracker mixture and mix until blended. Spoon the graham cracker mixture into the prepared pan and spread evenly. Using a rubber spatula, spread the rest of the chocolate mixture evenly over the mixture in the baking pan.

Chill the pan for 30 minutes, or until the chocolate is set. When ready to slice, remove from the pan and cut into equal-size squares for serving.

Cherry Pecan Bars

I love the pairing of fruit and nuts . . . it is truly a match made in heaven. For these bars, the combination of cherry and pecan has never tasted better. The tart flavor of the cherries works well with the nuttiness of the caramelly pecans, and the white chocolate brings it all together in this complete sweet treat, perfect for this holiday season!

Makes 1½ dozen bars

2 cups all-purpose flour

1½ cups granulated sugar, divided

¾ cup unsalted butter, at room temperature, plus 3 tablespoons melted for the egg mixture

4 large eggs

1 cup light corn syrup

1¼ cups pecans, finely chopped

¾ cup dried cherries, chopped

2 ounces white chocolate chips

Preheat the oven to 350°F. Oil a 9 x 13-inch baking pan and then cover it with parchment paper cut large enough to allow the paper to hang over all the sides. In a large bowl, combine the flour, ½ cup of the sugar, and butter, and mix until it comes together like crumbly bits of crust. Drop the dough into the prepared baking pan and firmly press it down, spreading it evenly over the bottom of the pan. Bake the crust for 17 to 20 minutes, until it is slightly puffed. Remove from the oven and set aside to cool slightly while you make the filling.

In a separate large bowl, combine the eggs, the remaining cup of sugar, corn syrup, and melted butter and mix well until everything comes together. Add the pecans and dried cherries and mix well. Gently spoon this mixture evenly over the crust and bake for 30 to 33 minutes, or until the filling is slightly firm and set. Remove from the oven.

Once the pan is cool, slice into bars. To finish the bars, melt the white chocolate chips in a microwave-safe bowl in the microwave or in the top of a double boiler until it is thin enough to pour. Drizzle each bar with a bit of white chocolate and let sit for 30 minutes to harden the chocolate before serving.

CHAPTER THREE

EDIBLE GIFTS & CANDIES

Festive English Toffee

Since I was a kid, I have always been obsessed with cooking. I loved eating the English toffee in candy boxes especially during the holidays. I never attempted to make it until I found myself frozen in front of the big candy store window on Main Street USA in Disneyland, my eyes glued to the candy maker preparing its famous English toffee. This is such a beloved holiday candy! Perfect with any combination of nuts and chocolate, it is sure to please any crowd and is really simple to prepare.

Makes 2 to 3 dozen pieces

1 cup unsalted butter

1¼ cups granulated sugar

¼ cup water

¼ cup light corn syrup

1 tablespoon pure vanilla extract

8 ounces semisweet chocolate chips

½ cup pecans, coarsely chopped

Line a baking sheet with parchment paper. In a large saucepan, combine the butter, sugar, water, corn syrup, and vanilla. Cook over medium heat, stirring just until the sugar melts. Let the mixture continue to cook undisturbed for 15 minutes, or until its temperature reaches 285°F on a candy thermometer. The mixture should achieve a light brown color.

Very carefully pour this onto the prepared cookie sheet. Sprinkle the chocolate chips on top and let them melt and soften, then use a spatula to spread the melted chocolate all over the toffee, covering every inch of it. Sprinkle with pecan pieces while the chocolate is still warm. Let the toffee set up and cool for 1 hour or more, then cut or break into pieces.

Peanut Butter Fudge

With only four simple ingredients, you are always minutes away from whipping up a fresh batch of this fudge. Deliciously smooth and full of peanut butter flavor, this is a great fudge to make during the holiday season, perfect for serving on a plate or platter or wrapping with a bow as a celebratory gesture. Everyone will love this delicious version of a classic sweet treat!

Makes 2 to 3 dozen pieces

1¼ cups unsalted butter

1¼ cups smooth peanut butter

1½ teaspoons pure vanilla extract

4½ cups powdered sugar

Line a square 8-inch baking pan with foil. In a medium-size saucepan, combine the butter and peanut butter and cook over medium heat, stirring often, until the mixture comes to a boil. Add the vanilla and powdered sugar and stir until well combined and smooth.

Pour the fudge mixture into the prepared baking pan and smooth the top with a spatula. Tap the baking pan on the counter to remove any bubbles from the inside, then cover with plastic wrap directly on the surface of the fudge and refrigerate for 1 hour or longer. Once it is set, cut into squares before serving.

"Christmas is doing a little something extra for someone."
—Charles M. Schulz

Rum Balls

Here is another holiday staple for our family during the holidays. These delicious balls are a burst of flavor that will leave you feeling perfectly satisfied. Vanilla wafers make this treat easy to make. You can skip the coconut garnish and roll the balls in cocoa powder for an even richer flavor. And with any garnish variation, don't be surprised when these disappear quickly!

Makes 2 to 3 dozen balls

5 cups crushed vanilla wafers (about 150 wafers)

2 cups ground walnuts

2 cups powdered sugar

1 teaspoon salt

½ cup unsweetened cocoa powder

1 cup rum

¼ cup plus 2 tablespoons honey

Fine coconut flakes, for coating

In a large bowl, combine the crushed vanilla wafers, walnuts, powdered sugar, salt, and cocoa. Add the rum and honey and stir to combine. Shape the dough into 1-inch balls, then drop and roll into coconut flakes. Serve immediately or store in an airtight container in the refrigerator until ready to enjoy; thaw before serving.

"I will honour Christmas in my heart, and try to keep it all the year."
—Charles Dickens

Peppermint Chocolate Bark

You know the season when you have peppermint bark! Nothing says "Christmastime" quite like this sweet treat! The combination of white chocolate and crushed candy canes does wonders. And for an even more decorated bark, try drizzling the top with a bit of milk chocolate for a perfect chocolate trifecta of flavor. Your guests will turn into true believers of Santa with a bit of this festive holiday candy.

Makes about 10 pieces

6 ounces dark chocolate

6 ounces white chocolate

¼ cup crushed peppermint sticks

Spray an 8-inch square baking pan with cooking spray, then line it with parchment paper.

Place the dark chocolate in a microwave-safe bowl and melt it in the microwave for 30 seconds. Remove the chocolate from the microwave to give it a quick stir and then place in the microwave for another 30 seconds, or until the chocolate is smooth when stirred. Alternatively, melt the chocolate in the top of a double boiler until smooth. Pour the melted dark chocolate into the prepared pan, using a spatula to spread it evenly. Gently tap the bottom of the pan onto the countertop a few times to remove any bubbles.

Melt the white chocolate, using the directions above. Once the white chocolate is smooth and silky, pour it on top of the dark chocolate and spread it evenly to match the thickness of the dark chocolate layer.

While the white chocolate is still warm, sprinkle the crushed peppermint sticks on top to make it look festive and decorated. Let the bark harden in the refrigerator for 2 hours, then slice it into squares for serving.

Easy Chocolate Truffles

I know what you're thinking: good truffles can only come from expensive French candy shops, right? No way, José . . . or shall I say no way, Josie! These delicious and super easy truffles are going to impress all your guests this holiday season. Your hands will get messy during the process, but it will all be worth it in the end.

Makes 1 to 2 dozen pieces

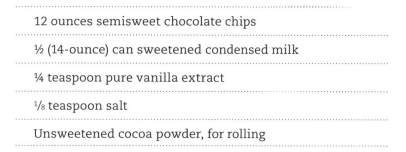

12 ounces semisweet chocolate chips

½ (14-ounce) can sweetened condensed milk

¼ teaspoon pure vanilla extract

⅛ teaspoon salt

Unsweetened cocoa powder, for rolling

Place the chocolate in a microwave-safe bowl and melt in the microwave for 30 seconds. Remove from the microwave and quickly stir. If the chocolate is not melted all the way, microwave for another 30 seconds, or until it is smooth. Alternatively, melt the chocolate in the top of a double boiler until smooth, and transfer to a medium-size bowl.

Stir the condensed milk, vanilla, and salt into the melted chocolate and mix well. Place the mixture in the refrigerator to firm up. Once it is cool, shape into 1-inch truffle balls. Finally, roll your truffles in cocoa powder and serve on a platter to your guests.

Holiday Chocolate Fudge

I've taken this classic dessert and have made it new and festive for this special time of year! You've got to try this recipe! This delicious holiday take on chocolate fudge will satisfy any chocolate cravings you have, and the contrast of candy cane bits is beautiful and delicious. This is the perfect way to showcase the best flavors of this celebratory season.

Makes 1 dozen pieces

24 ounces dark chocolate, chopped

1 (14-ounce) can sweetened condensed milk

3 tablespoons unsalted butter

½ teaspoon peppermint extract

¼ cup crushed peppermint candy canes

Line a 9-inch square baking pan with foil and grease the bottom and sides with cooking spray. In a saucepan, combine the dark chocolate, sweetened condensed milk, and butter. Cook over medium heat, stirring, until everything melts together. Remove from the heat and stir in the peppermint extract.

Pour the fudge into the prepared baking pan, then sprinkle the crushed candy canes on top. Allow the fudge to set and cool for 1 hour before cutting into squares.

Christmas Caramel Corn

A family holiday tradition in our house, this foolproof caramel corn is a festive addition to your holiday sweet treat offering. You'll make a batch and it will be gone faster than you can make another. My Auntie Rie makes this caramel corn the best and I mean, THE BEST. She's perfected this recipe and together we wanted to share this recipe with you, so here you have it!

Makes 6 to 8 quarts caramel corn

6 to 8 quarts popped popcorn (popped on the stove with 2 tablespoons oil)

1 cup unsalted butter, at room temperature

2 cups packed light brown sugar

½ cup light corn syrup

1 teaspoon salt

1 teaspoon pure vanilla extract

2 teaspoons baking soda

Preheat the oven to 250°F. Spread all the popped popcorn in a large roasting pan (can be a disposable pan), making sure to remove any unpopped kernels.

In a medium-size saucepan, mix together the butter, brown sugar, corn syrup, and salt. Stir over low heat until the butter is melted, then bring to a boil, stirring constantly. Continuing to stir constantly, boil for 5 minutes. Remove from the heat and quickly add the vanilla and baking soda. Carefully mix until the caramel reaches a medium brown-colored foam that has doubled in size. Immediately pour the mixture over the popcorn and stir well.

Bake for 1 hour, stirring and coating the popcorn every 15 minutes, making sure to cover all the popcorn with the caramel. Remove from the oven and pour the popcorn onto waxed paper to cool, breaking apart any large clumps before storing or serving.

CHAPTER FOUR

SWEET HOLIDAY CLASSICS

Eggnog & Poppy Seed Cake

Here's a delicious and easy-to-make cake that brings the flavors of the holiday season to one simple and satisfying dessert. If you are looking for something to prepare that is quick, casual, and all-around tasty, this is the recipe for you! Bold poppy seed flavor, bright citrus, and rich eggnog come together nicely with this yummy cake that has tons of character.

Makes 10 servings

2½ cups all-purpose flour

1 cup granulated sugar

¼ cup poppy seeds

1¼ cups eggnog

1 tablespoon orange zest

3 tablespoons vegetable oil

1 teaspoon orange extract

3½ teaspoons baking powder

1 teaspoon salt

1 teaspoon freshly grated nutmeg

1 large egg

Preheat the oven to 350°F. Grease a 9 x 13-inch baking pan with cooking spray. In a large bowl, beat together all of the ingredients.

Pour the cake batter into the prepared baking pan and bake for 22 to 25 minutes, or until a toothpick inserted into the center comes out clean. Remove from the oven and let it cool slightly before slicing.

Pumpkin Cheesecake

You can't have Christmas without a pumpkin cheesecake, right? At least that's the way I feel! Try this recipe and you will realize just how easy it is to make one of the most adored classic American holiday desserts. Smooth, delicious pumpkin and cream cheese harmonize beautifully together. This is a perfect ending to any of your holiday meals this time of year.

Makes 8 servings

CRUST:

2 cups graham cracker crumbs

3 tablespoons unsalted butter, melted

2 tablespoons granulated sugar

FILLING:

2 large eggs

2 (8-ounce) packages cream cheese, softened

1 teaspoon pure vanilla extract

¾ cup granulated sugar

1 (15-ounce) can pure pumpkin purée

2¾ teaspoons pumpkin pie spice

Preheat the oven to 350°F. Start by making the crust: In a medium-size mixing bowl, mix together the graham cracker crumbs, melted butter, and sugar. Press the mixture evenly into the bottom and sides of a 9-inch springform pan then set aside while you prepare the filling.

For the filling, in a large bowl, combine the eggs, cream cheese, vanilla, and sugar and mix well until smooth. Once the mixture is smooth, add the pumpkin purée and pumpkin pie spice and mix until well combined.

Spoon the filling into the piecrust and bake for 38 to 45 minutes, or until set. Remove from the oven and let cool before slicing and serving.

Tip: Pumpkin pie spice is a combination of classic baking spices and can be found in the spice section of most supermarkets and specialty markets.

Vanilla Meringues

If you've never made meringues before, I would encourage you to give it a try! Light and airy, these meringues add a touch of delicate elegance to your offering at Christmastime. These are a perfectly sweet yet subtle treat that looks so festive on a platter served to your guests. Whip up these delicious vanilla meringues for the holidays and voilà!

Makes 12 to 18 meringues

4 large egg whites, at room temperature

⅛ teaspoon cream of tartar

¼ teaspoon salt

1 teaspoon pure vanilla extract

1 cup superfine sugar

Preheat the oven to 200°F. Line a baking sheet with parchment paper. In the bowl of a stand mixer fitted with a whisk attachment, beat together the egg whites, cream of tartar, salt, and vanilla until soft peaks form. At this point, gradually add half the sugar and continue to whisk until stiff peaks form, then add the remaining sugar.

Spoon this mixture into a resealable plastic bag. Gently push all the mixture to one lower corner of the bag, then snip off a ½-inch piece of the corner to make a piping bag.

Pipe small meringue mounds 1 inch apart onto the prepared pan, using up all of the mixture. Bake the meringues until hard, about 2 hours. They should easily release from the parchment. Turn off the oven, prop the door open, and allow the meringues to sit in the oven for another hour to cool.

Holiday Trifle

Trifles are so fun to build and simply gorgeous to present to your family and friends. This holiday version is just as delicious as any other, with big chunks of angel food cake and raspberries that dance together in this stunning dessert. Try it with any combination of berries that you like for an easy-to-make dessert that will be a showpiece on your Christmas table.

Makes 8 servings

5 cups fresh raspberries

¼ cup granulated sugar

Juice of ½ orange

4 cups heavy whipping cream

¼ cup powdered sugar

2 teaspoons pure vanilla extract

1 (17-ounce) store-bought angel food cake

In a medium-size nonreactive bowl, combine the raspberries, granulated sugar, and orange juice and let macerate for 10 minutes.

Meanwhile, in a large bowl, combine the cream and powdered sugar and whisk vigorously until stiff peaks appear. It may take 8 to 10 minutes to achieve a fully whipped cream. Add the vanilla and mix quickly once more to incorporate.

Cut the angel food cake into large chunks, then begin to build your trifle. Start by adding about one-third of the cake chunks to the bottom of a trifle dish or other clear, straight-sided glass serving dish. Add a layer of the syrupy berries and then a layer of whipped cream. Repeat to make one more layer of each and top the trifle with a few extra raspberries for garnish.

Hot Cocoa with Whipped Cream

Homemade cocoa is so simple and so special this time of year. There's nothing like the power of hot cocoa to transport you back in time to when you were a kid. And I know it's not just your kid that loves cocoa; everyone, young and small, loves this classic heart-warming drink. You know its wintertime when you start to crave hot cocoa!

Makes 4 cups cocoa

½ cup heavy whipping cream

3 tablespoons powdered sugar

¼ cup unsweetened cocoa powder

4 tablespoons granulated sugar

6 cups whole milk

1 teaspoon pure vanilla extract

6 ounces milk chocolate, chopped, plus ½ ounce grated for garnish

In a medium-size bowl, make the whipped cream by whisking the cream and powdered sugar together until stiff peaks form.

In a small bowl, combine the cocoa powder and granulated sugar and mix well. In a medium-size pot, heat the milk over medium heat, stirring constantly, until the milk just begins to boil, and then turn off the heat.

Place 3 tablespoons of the cocoa mixture in a separate small bowl then stir in a bit of the hot milk to create a paste. Reheat the remaining milk over medium heat, then mix in the cocoa paste and whisk until fully incorporated. Add the vanilla and 6 ounces of chocolate chunks and stir until the chocolate is melted. Carefully pour into mugs and top with whipped cream and a garnish of the last ½ ounce of grated chocolate on top.

Christmas Morning Cinnamon Buns

Wake up to presents under the tree and these delicious buns in the oven. The aroma of sweet cinnamon will waft through your whole house. And once they are ready to eat, the presents can wait! There's something about watching the expression on people's faces when they are enthralled in what they are eating. It's pure joy. Home-made cinnamon rolls do that to people.

Makes 1 dozen buns

¼ cup plus 2 tablespoons granulated sugar

1 teaspoon salt

½ cup unsalted butter, at room temperature, divided

1 large egg, beaten

1 teaspoon pure vanilla extract

3½ cups all-purpose flour

2 teaspoons instant dry active yeast

1¼ cups whole milk

6½ tablespoons granulated sugar mixed with 1½ tablespoons ground cinnamon

In the bowl of a stand mixer fitted with the paddle attachment, combine the sugar, salt, and 6 tablespoons of the butter and mix on medium speed until everything is fluffy and smooth. Add the egg and vanilla and mix until well combined, then add the flour, yeast, and milk and mix until a dough ball forms.

Lay the dough on a lightly floured work surface and knead it for 10 minutes, or until soft and supple. Transfer the dough to a greased bowl, cover it with a damp kitchen towel, and set aside in a warm spot in your kitchen to rise for 2 hours, or until the dough doubles its size.

Line a 9 x 13-inch baking pan with parchment paper. Lay the dough on your lightly floured work surface and roll it out to a 12 x 14-inch rectangle. Melt the remaining 2 tablespoons of butter and brush it over the dough, then sprinkle evenly with the cinnamon-sugar mixture. Starting from the short end, gently roll the dough into a log and place it seam side down on your work surface. Using a sharp knife, slice the dough into 12 equal portions and place in the prepared baking pan with 3 inches of space between each bun. Let the buns rise again for 1½ hours, or until they have doubled in size.

Preheat the oven to 350°F. Once the oven is hot, bake the cinnamon buns for 22 to 25 minutes, or until they are just golden brown. Remove them from the oven and serve warm.

Chocolate Pudding Cake

Try this vintage holiday dessert for a new take on an old classic. Chocolate pudding cake used to be a common dessert for the Christmas table, and with this delicious recipe you will wonder why you haven't made it every year past. This simple and delicious steamed pudding is cooked to moist perfection and is a delicious dessert for any meal throughout the holiday season.

Makes 4 to 6 servings

1 cup all-purpose flour

1 teaspoon baking powder

¼ teaspoon salt

3 tablespoons unsweetened cocoa powder, divided

4 tablespoons unsalted butter, at room temperature

¾ cup light brown sugar

2 large eggs

1 teaspoon pure vanilla extract

½ teaspoon rum extract

½ cup whole milk

4 ounces dark chocolate, chopped

1 cup raisins

¼ cup granulated sugar

¼ cup water

1 tablespoon powdered sugar

Place a small or medium-size heatproof dinner plate in the bottom of a stock-pot. Generously butter a 2½-cup heatproof glass bowl (about 3 inches deep by 5 inches wide), then place the bowl in the stockpot on top of the plate and add enough water to the stockpot to come up to the side of the bowl just past the halfway point. Place over medium-high heat to begin boiling the water.

In a medium-size bowl, sift together the flour, baking powder, and salt, and mix in 2 tablespoons of the cocoa powder. In a separate large bowl, cream together the butter and brown sugar until fluffy and smooth, then add the eggs, vanilla, and rum extract and mix well. Gradually add the flour mixture and milk to the butter mixture and mix just until everything is well blended. Melt the chocolate in a microwave-safe bowl in the microwave or in the top of a double boiler just until it is smooth, then add to the batter along with the raisins and gently fold until everything is well combined.

Pour the batter into the prepared glass bowl (your pudding mold) and cover the stockpot with its lid. Simmer for 1½ hours, peeking into the pot occasionally: You must avoid letting any water get into the mold while boil-ing and ensure that the pudding mold does not touch the bottom of the pot and remains standing upright and straight throughout the steaming process. Every 30 minutes, check the water and add a bit more to the pot to keep the water level consistent during the entire 2½ hours.

At the end of the steaming time, carefully remove the glass bowl with the pudding mold from the pot and let it sit for 5 minutes while you prepare the glaze. In a saucepan, combine the remaining tablespoon of cocoa powder, granulated sugar, and water over high heat and bring to a boil. Once it boils, let it simmer for a few minutes, then remove from the heat.

Invert the pudding onto a cooling rack positioned over a baking sheet. While the pudding is still warm, brush the chocolate glaze all over the pud-ding, then dust with powdered sugar and carefully transfer to a serving plate and serve warm.

Homemade Eggnog

Eggnog has never tasted so good! Try this simple and delicious version of home-made eggnog and you'll never buy store-bought again! The rich flavor of cream and nutmeg will warm you up this winter season. And if you want to be even toastier, try adding a splash of peppermint schnapps, spiced rum, or bourbon for an even tastier holiday treat!

Makes 3 to 5 servings

1 cup granulated sugar

½ teaspoon salt

6 large eggs

3 cups milk

1 cup heavy whipping cream

½ teaspoon pure vanilla extract

Freshly grated nutmeg

In a medium-size bowl, mix together the granulated sugar and salt. Add the eggs and whisk until everything is very well-blended. Pour the milk into a pot and simmer over medium heat, stirring constantly, for 2 minutes. Slowly pour the egg mixture into the milk while whisking and whisk continuously for about 5 minutes, or until the mixture just begins to simmer. The mixture should begin to thicken and become smooth. You will know it is done when it coats the back of a spoon.

Take the pot off the heat as soon as the proper consistency is reached, then add the cream and vanilla and stir to combine. Serve the eggnog warm or chilled and with a dusting of nutmeg.

Grandma's Famous Gelatin Mold

You're not going to believe me when I say this, but Jell-O mold is my favorite part of every Christmas meal. Yes, I know. I'm a chef so I should love the spiral ham, glazed turkey, or scallop potatoes, and believe me I do . . . but Jell-O mold is a must for me. This is an elegant version of the classic Christmas dinner staple that my Grandma Millie makes every year. This can be served with dinner or after dinner, and will be the most loved dish on the table either way. Thanks for introducing me to something so delicious, Grandma!

Makes 10 to 12 servings

2 (3-ounce) packages raspberry Jell-O

2 cups hot water

1 (12-ounce) bag frozen raspberries, thawed

1 (12-ounce) bag frozen blueberries, thawed

½ cup crushed pineapple (with juice)

1½ cups sour cream

In a large bowl, dissolve the Jell-O in the hot water. Stir in the thawed berries and pineapple (with its juice). Pour the mixture into a large gelatin mold or a 9 x 13-inch glass pan and chill until firm.

Carefully unmold the Jell-O by inverting it onto a serving platter or plate. Garnish the center with chilled sour cream. Make sure when you serve this that each guest gets a bit of sour cream with each slice of the Jell-O!

Mini Sherry Wine Cakes

This recipe is so easy and so darn delicious. These festive little cakes are a great addition to your holiday baked goods. In this recipe, classic yellow cake meets sherry wine and it's never tasted better. You can bake these as individual cakes as written, or bake this as one large cake if you would rather have larger slices. Either way, this is a recipe you'll want to keep in your back pocket.

Makes 8 to 10 servings

1 (15¼-ounce) package yellow cake mix

1 (3½-ounce) package vanilla instant pudding

¾ cup vegetable oil

¾ cup sherry

4 large eggs

Powdered sugar

Preheat the oven to 350°F. Generously grease and flour three mini Bundt pans. In a large bowl, combine the cake mix, instant vanilla pudding, oil, sherry, and eggs and mix well.

Divide the batter evenly among the prepared Bundt pans and bake for 22 to 24 minutes, or until the cakes spring back when touched. Remove from the oven and let cool for 5 to 10 minutes. If using a larger pan, bake the cake for 45 minutes.

Use a knife to loosen each cake from around its pan and use your palm to catch the cake in your hand once it releases itself. Gently place the cakes on a cooling rack. Once cool, sprinkle generously with sifted powdered sugar before serving.

Glazed Pumpkin Bundt Cake

Perfectly moist and full of the season's most beloved spices complemented by a creamy glaze, this Bundt cake is a winner. This recipe is a great way to use up canned pumpkin purée and is a wonderful dessert that works well after a casual or sophisticated meal or for a holiday brunch or breakfast offering.

Makes 10 to 12 servings

¾ cup butter at room temperature, plus more for pan

1½ cups granulated sugar

3 large eggs, beaten

1¼ cups pumpkin purée

3 cups all-purpose flour

1 teaspoon baking powder

1 teaspoon baking soda

½ teaspoon salt

4 teaspoons pumpkin pie spice

1 cup buttermilk

GLAZE:

1 cup granulated sugar

2 tablespoons unsalted butter, at room temperature

½ cup heavy whipping cream

¼ cup pecans

Preheat the oven to 350°F and butter a Bundt pan. In a bowl, cream together the sugar and butter until fluffy and smooth. Add the eggs and pumpkin purée and mix to combine. In a separate medium-size bowl, combine the flour, baking powder, baking soda, salt, and pumpkin pie spice and mix together. Gradually add the flour mixture and buttermilk to the butter mixture and mix just until everything is well combined.

Pour the batter into the prepared pan and bake for about 45 minutes, or until a toothpick inserted into the center comes out clean. Remove the cake from the oven and let cool completely before turning it out of the pan.

For the glaze, heat the sugar in a medium-size pan over medium heat until the sugar turns golden and is completely melted. Add the butter and cream and stir constantly for 10 minutes over low heat, or until you have a smooth caramel glaze. Add the pecans, stir to coat, then gently pour the glaze over the top of the Bundt cake and serve.

Tip: Pumpkin pie spice is a combination of classic baking spices and can be found in the spice section of most supermarkets and specialty stores.

Index